INSIDE MEN'S COLLEGE BASKETBALL™

BASKETBALL IN THE BIG EAST CONFERENCE

rosen publishing's
rosen central®

JASON PORTERFIELD

New York

Published in 2008 by The Rosen Publishing Group, Inc.
29 East 21st Street, New York, NY 10010

Library of Congress Cataloging-in-Publication Data

Porterfield, Jason.
Basketball in the Big East Conference / Jason Porterfield. — 1st ed.
   p. cm. — (Inside men's college basketball)
Includes bibliographical references and index.
ISBN-13: 978-1-4042-1381-4 (library binding)
1. Big East Conference—History. 2. Basketball—Tournaments—United States—
History. 3. College sports—East (U.S.)—History. I. Title.
GV885.415.B54P67 2008
796.323'630973—dc22

                       2007028627

Manufactured in the United States of America

On the cover: *(Top)* The Pittsburgh Panthers men's basketball team rallies before a game in 2005. *(Bottom)* Syracuse's Carmelo Anthony attempts a shot over Georgetown's Michael Sweetney in a 2003 Big East matchup.

CONTENTS

INTRODUCTION

In 2003, the Syracuse Orangemen faced off against Kansas University in the championship game of the NCAA tournament, the most important game in college basketball. Kansas trailed by eight points but roared back in the final minutes to make the score 78–81. With 1.5 seconds left, Kansas player Michael Lee attempted a three-point shot that would tie the game. But Syracuse star Hakim Warrick hustled over, his long arm outstretched . . . blocked! Warrick's great defensive play sealed Syracuse's first national championship. The championship win was the fourth for a team from the Big East, one of the NCAA's most successful conferences.

The National Collegiate Athletic Association (NCAA) oversees college sports and is the largest intercollegiate organization in

The Pittsburgh Panthers and Georgetown Hoyas face off in the first game of the 2007 Big East tournament, held annually at New York City's Madison Square Garden.

the world. Its membership includes colleges and universities of all kinds, as well as a number of athletic conferences and local and regional sporting organizations. Every year, the NCAA awards eighty-eight national championships in sporting events for men and women. The organization also draws up and enforces the rules of play for twelve sports, including men's college basketball. Big East teams have been a constant presence in the NCAA basketball championship tournament since the conference's founding.

In basketball, sixty-four NCAA Division I teams qualify to play in the championship tournament. After several rounds of games, the two teams that remain undefeated play each other in the final game. The winning team is named NCAA champion, the best team in college basketball.

1 CHAPTER

NCAA Basketball and the Big East

The National Collegiate Athletic Association was founded in 1906. The organization's first national basketball tournament took place in 1939, when the University of Oregon defeated Ohio State University. The tournament initially featured the top teams from eight regions across the country. Over time, the tournament field grew to sixty-four teams. These include the champions of each Division I athletic conference, as well as "at-large" teams chosen by the NCAA selection committee. Today, the exciting tournament is known as March Madness, since most of the games are played in that month.

The tournament rounds grow increasingly prestigious as winning teams advance. The third round is called the Sweet Sixteen, for the sixteen teams still alive. The fourth round is called the Elite Eight. The Final Four teams play in the semifinal games, with the two winners advancing to the championship game. When teams advance into the later rounds, it reflects positively on the players and coaches as well as the schools they represent. It also raises the profile of the athletic conference the teams play in.

The Big East: A Basketball Conference

The Big East formed in 1979. At that time, the athletic directors from Providence College, St. John's University, Syracuse University, and Georgetown University got together to develop a conference that would focus on basketball, rather than some other collegiate sport. They invited Seton Hall University, the University of

Georgetown Hoyas legend Patrick Ewing shoots during a 1985 game against the Syracuse Orangemen. Syracuse and Georgetown were among the group of teams that formed the Big East.

Connecticut, and Boston College to join them, creating the Big East Conference. Villanova University joined in 1980, followed by the University of Pittsburgh in 1982.

The first Big East tournament was held in 1980, with Georgetown beating Syracuse. Two years later, Georgetown became the first Big East team to advance to the NCAA championship game. (Georgetown lost the game to the University of North Carolina.) Then, in 1984, Georgetown defeated Houston in the NCAA championship game, giving the Big East its first men's basketball championship. Many other NCAA tournament successes followed, building the Big East's reputation as one of the best college basketball conferences in the country.

The Big East expanded rapidly during the 1990s. The University of Miami's basketball team joined in 1991, followed by the University of Notre Dame, Rutgers University, and West Virginia University in 1995, and Virginia Tech in 2000. College basketball is a big business, and successful and competitive teams can be a financial boon to an athletic conference. For this reason, the Atlantic Coast Conference (ACC) created a controversy in 2003, when it tried to lure schools away from the Big East. Several Big East schools sued the ACC to prevent the move, but the conference realignment went through anyway. In the end, Miami and Virginia Tech left to join the ACC in 2004, followed by Boston College in 2005. The Big East made up for the loss of the three teams by inviting five schools from Conference USA to join: DePaul University, Marquette University, and the universities of Louisville, Cincinnati, and South Florida all became Big East members in 2005.

The Big East Outgrows the East

As of 2007, the Big East had sixteen member schools, making it the largest Division I-A college athletic conference. The seven original Big East teams all were located in the northeastern United States. With the recent expansion, however, the conference has grown to include schools in the Southeast and Midwest. Big East schools are located in Connecticut (UConn), Washington, D.C. (Georgetown), Rhode Island (Providence), Pennsylvania (Villanova and Pittsburgh), New York (Syracuse and St. John's), New Jersey (Seton Hall and Rutgers), Illinois (DePaul), Indiana (Notre Dame), Florida (South Florida), West Virginia (West Virginia), Kentucky (Louisville), Ohio (Cincinnati), and Wisconsin (Marquette).

University of Connecticut players celebrate their 2004 NCAA tournament championship. The Huskies defeated the Georgia Tech Yellow Jackets in the final game, 82–73.

The Big East Season

Each season, Big East teams play sixteen games against other teams in the conference to determine the league standings. Each school's schedule includes "mirror" games against three conference opponents who are played in home and away games in a season. On a rotating schedule, ten of the other twelve conference teams are played once in the season. (Two teams are skipped entirely.)

SCHOOL	TEAM NAME	YEAR JOINED BIG EAST	BIG EAST REGULAR SEASON CONFERENCE CHAMPIONSHIPS	BIG EAST TOURNAMENT TITLES	NCAA TOURNAMENT APPEARANCES
Cincinnati	Bearcats	2005	0	0	24
Connecticut	Huskies	1979	10	6	27
DePaul	Blue Demons	2005	0	0	22
Georgetown	Hoyas	1979	5	7	24
Louisville	Cardinals	2005	0	0	33
Marquette	Golden Eagles	2005	0	0	25
Notre Dame	Fighting Irish	1995	1	0	28
Pittsburgh	Panthers	1982	4	1	19
Providence	Friars	1979	0	1	15
Rutgers	Scarlet Knights	1995	0	0	6
St. John's	Red Storm	1979	3	3	27
Seton Hall	Pirates	1979	2	2	9
South Florida	Bulls	2005	0	0	2
Syracuse	Orange	1979	7	5	31
Villanova	Wildcats	1980	3	1	28
West Virginia	Mountaineers	1995	0	0	20

At the end of the season, the top twelve teams in the Big East compete in the Big East tournament. Every year since 1983, the tournament has been played at New York City's famed Madison Square Garden. The tournament's most outstanding player is awarded the Dave Gavitt Trophy—named for the conference's first

NCAA TOURNAMENT WINS/LOSSES (winning percentage)	NCAA FINAL FOUR APPEARANCES	NCAA CHAMPIONSHIPS	BIG EAST CONFERENCE PLAYERS OF THE YEAR	FIRST-ROUND NBA DRAFT PICKS
40–23 (.635)	6	2	0	12
42–26 (.618)	2	2	6	14
21–25 (.457)	2	0	0	11
44–23 (.657)	5	1	7	10
54–35 (.607)	8	2	0	18
32–26 (.552)	3	1	0	5
29–35 (.475)	1	0	3	19
17–20 (.460)	1	0	2	4
14–16 (.467)	2	0	0	9
5–7 (.417)	1	0	0	3
27–29 (.482)	2	0	4	15
15–9 (.625)	1	0	2	11
0–2 (.000)	1	0	0	0
48–31 (.608)	1	1	3	14
42–28 (.600)	1	1	2	11
18–20 (.474)	1	0	0	5

commissioner. The Big East recognizes a regular season champion for the team with the best conference record, but only the tournament champion gets an automatic bid to go to the NCAA tournament.

Coaching in the Big East

Big East coaches such as Syracuse's Jim Boeheim and Georgetown's John Thompson Jr. became basketball legends over the course of many seasons in the conference. Others, like Providence's Rick Pitino and Pittsburgh's Ben Howland, spent only a few years in the Big East before moving on to even greater success in other conferences. These men and some of the other popular and successful Big East coaches are profiled in this chapter.

John Thompson Jr.—Georgetown

John Thompson Jr. was head coach of the Georgetown Hoyas from 1972 to 1999. He inherited a team that had won just three games in 1971. Only three seasons later, he led the Hoyas to an 18–10 record and a bid in the 1975 NCAA tournament. The Hoyas would go

Legendary Georgetown Hoyas coach John Thompson Jr. congratulates his young star, Allen Iverson, after a game. Thompson's steady leadership helped make the Hoyas one of the Big East's most successful teams.

on to make twenty additional trips to the NCAA tournament under Thompson, including a streak of fourteen consecutive tournament appearances from 1979 to 1992. The Hoyas were NCAA champions in 1984, and runners-up in 1982 and 1985. Thompson was named Big East Coach of the Year three times, in 1980, 1987, and 1992. He retired in 1999, with a 596–239 coaching record. Thompson's son, John Thompson III, took over the head-coaching position at Georgetown in 2004.

Jim Calhoun—UConn

Jim Calhoun coached at Northeastern University from 1972 until accepting the head-coaching job at the University of Connecticut in 1986. In 1988, he led the Huskies to a National Invitational Tournament (NIT) championship. The program really burst on the scene in 1990, when UConn went 31–6, won the Big East, and made it to the Elite Eight. Calhoun's Huskies won the NCAA championship twice, in 1999 and 2004. Under Calhoun, Connecticut has won or shared the Big East regular season title ten times, won six Big East tournaments, and earned a 222–112 record in the Big East. Including his time at Northeastern, Calhoun has an impressive 750–328 career coaching record.

Jim Boeheim—Syracuse

Jim Boeheim has been head coach at Syracuse University since 1976. His teams have made twenty-five appearances in the NCAA tournament, including three trips to the Final Four (1987, 1996,

Dave Gavitt: Coach and Commissioner

Dave Gavitt was head coach at Providence from 1969 to 1979. As a coach, he led the Friars to five NCAA tournament appearances, including Providence's first Final Four, in 1973. From 1971 onward, he also acted as the school's athletic director. In that role, he was one of the administrators who decided to form the Big East in 1979. Gavitt became the conference's first commissioner and held that position until retiring in 1990. The conference's Dave Gavitt Trophy—awarded to the Big East tournament's most outstanding player—is named for him.

and 2003). His 2003 team, led by Carmelo Anthony, won the NCAA championship. Syracuse has won seven Big East regular season championships and five Big East tournament championships. Boeheim was named Big East Coach of the Year in 1984, 1991, and 2000. He leads all Big East coaches in conference wins with 291. His 750 career wins rank nineteenth in NCAA history.

Rick Pitino—Providence, Louisville

Coaching whiz Rick Pitino began his career in 1974, when he became an assistant coach at the University of Hawaii. From 1976 to 1978, he was an assistant coach at Syracuse; he went on to become

Syracuse coach Jim Boeheim instructs his team during the championship game of the 2003 NCAA tournament.

head coach at Boston University. Pitino then was Providence's head coach from 1985 to 1987, the year he led the Friars to the Final Four. After a brief stint coaching the New York Knicks in the National Basketball Association (NBA), Pitino became head coach at the University of Kentucky in 1989. He later led the Wildcats to the NCAA championship in 1996. Kentucky returned to the championship game the following year but lost to the University of Arizona. Pitino then left the college ranks again to coach the struggling Boston Celtics in the NBA.

In 2001, Pitino returned to NCAA basketball, taking over the program at Louisville. In 2005, he led the Cardinals to their first Final Four appearance in nineteen years. Pitino is the only men's college basketball coach in history to lead teams from three different schools to the Final Four. He has a 494–182 record as a college coach.

Ben Howland—Pittsburgh

Ben Howland coached at Pittsburgh from 1999 to 2003. Before his arrival, Pittsburgh's basketball program had been struggling for years. In 2000–2001, however, Howland led the team to a 19–14 record and an NIT appearance. In 2001–2002, Pittsburgh finished with a 27–5 regular season record and advanced to the Sweet Sixteen, earning Howland the Big East Coach of the Year Award. The following year, the Panthers won their first Big East tournament and returned to the Sweet Sixteen. Unfortunately for Pitt, Howland left after the 2002–2003 season to coach at UCLA. During his four seasons in the Big East, he compiled an 89–40 record.

Rollie Massimino—Villanova

Rollie Massimino coached at Villanova from 1973 to 1992. Before Villanova joined the Big East in 1980, Massimino's Wildcats played in the Eastern Eight Conference. They won three consecutive Eastern Eight Conference titles, from 1978 to 1980. Villanova also won Big East regular season titles in 1982 and 1983.

Massimino's Villanova teams made eleven NCAA tournament appearances, including five trips to the Elite Eight. In 1985, Massimino coached Villanova to their only NCAA championship, upsetting the heavily favored Georgetown Hoyas, 66–64. Massimino was the Big East Coach of the Year that season. He owns a 357–241 coaching record at Villanova and a 515–391 career coaching record.

P. J. Carlesimo —Seton Hall

As Seton Hall's coach from 1982 to 1994, P. J. Carlesimo put together a 212–166 record. In 1988, Carlesimo coached the Pirates to their first-ever NCAA tournament appearance. They would make five more trips to the tournament under Carlesimo, including a 1989 tournament run that saw them advance to the championship

Wildcats players lift coach Rollie Massimino after the team's stunning 66–64 upset of Georgetown in the 1985 NCAA final.

game before losing to Michigan in overtime. Seton Hall named Carlesimo their "Coach of the Century."

Mike Brey—Notre Dame

Mike Brey took over the head-coach position at Notre Dame in 2000. In his first season, Brey led the school to the 2001 NCAA tournament, its first tournament appearance since 1990. Notre Dame also won

Notre Dame coach Mike Brey encourages his team from the sidelines during the 2007 Big East tournament. Brey's arrival helped to revive Notre Dame's once-great basketball program.

their first regular season Big East championship in 2001, going 11–5 in conference games. The team returned to the NCAA tournament in 2002 and 2003, making it to the Sweet Sixteen in 2003. Brey was named Big East Coach of the Year in 2007, after another trip to the tournament. As of 2007, Brey had 141 wins with Notre Dame and a 240–128 coaching record overall.

3 CHAPTER

Big East Competition

Since the creation of the Big East in 1979, its teams have been among the most competitive in college basketball. With its strong programs, Big East basketball quickly developed great conference rivalries. These rivalries have played out during the regular season, in supercompetitive Big East tournament games, and even in NCAA tournament matchups. Conference expansion has introduced new rivalries as well.

Conference Rivalries

Georgetown's early success—the Hoyas won six of the first ten Big East tournaments—guaranteed that rivalries would develop with other dominant conference schools. Geography also has played a part in rivalries, particularly between the two New Jersey schools, Rutgers and Seton Hall.

West Virginia fans overrun the court after the Mountaineers upset highly ranked Pittsburgh in a 2006 game at West Virginia. The two teams' long-standing football rivalry is now a hoops rivalry as well.

Georgetown and Syracuse have been rivals from the very beginning. In 1980, Georgetown broke Syracuse's fifty-seven-game home winning streak. Making the loss sting even more, it was the last game the Orange played on their old home court, the Manley Field House. Over the years, Georgetown coach John Thompson Jr. and Syracuse coach Jim Boeheim helped build the rivalry by leading two of the conference's most dominant teams. Fans of both schools have joined in the spirit, from local Syracuse banks handing out pins that mock the Hoyas' nickname, to

Georgetown fans stealing a Syracuse cheerleaders' "SU" sign and changing it to read "GU."

During the 1980s, Georgetown, Syracuse, and St. John's had nationally ranked programs, which led to great contests. The Georgetown–Syracuse rivalry is still probably the most intense in the conference. Recently, however, both teams have built rivalries with Connecticut, which won the NCAA championship in 1999 and 2004. Syracuse, for its part, was crowned NCAA champ in 2003.

Rutgers and Seton Hall have the two largest athletics programs in New Jersey. Their rivalry faded somewhat as both teams declined during the late 1990s but began to revive in 2007. That January, Rutgers—which had lost five straight games to Seton Hall—beat the Pirates in double overtime at home, stunning Seton Hall fans who had gotten used to chanting "We own Jersey" after each game.

Since 2002, Pittsburgh and Connecticut have been two of the most successful Big East teams, building an intense rivalry based on that success. In that time, they've played each other twelve times, splitting the series 6–6. The teams competed against each other in three consecutive Big East tournament championship games. The 2002 championship game between them ended with Connecticut winning in double overtime. Pittsburgh beat Connecticut in the 2003 final to win its first Big East title, while Connecticut returned the favor in 2004, beating Pittsburgh 61–58.

The Big East Championship Tournament

Since 1980, nine different schools have won the Big East tournament. Georgetown leads with seven titles, six of them coming in the conference's first ten years. Connecticut has won six times, while

Chris Mullin and Walter Berry help carry
a jubilant coach Lou Carnesecca after
St. John's upset win over Syracuse in
the 1986 Big East tournament.

Syracuse has five wins and St. John's has three. Seton Hall has won twice, and Providence, Villanova, and Pittsburgh each have won once. Of the teams that have won the Big East tournament, the Georgetown Hoyas (1984) and the Connecticut Huskies (1999, 2004) went on to win the NCAA championship.

The first Big East tournament took place in 1980. John Thompson Jr.'s Georgetown Hoyas faced the Syracuse Orangemen. Led by Big East Player of the Year John Duren and tournament MVP Craig Shelton, Georgetown beat Syracuse 87–81. The win was the first of Thompson's six Big East titles. His Hoyas advanced to the Elite Eight that year.

In 1986, Syracuse advanced to the tournament against St. John's. The Orangemen already had beaten St. John's during the regular season, with Syracuse player Dwayne "Pearl" Washington handing out eighteen assists in one game. Syracuse led in the tournament game until the final seconds, when a jump shot by Ron Rowan gave St. John's a 70–69 lead. With Syracuse in possession of the ball, Washington drove to the hoop for what looked like a game-winning layup. But St. John's star Walter Berry blocked the shot, stunning Washington and sealing the win for St. John's.

Georgetown and Syracuse played each other in the 1992 Big East championship game. Over the years, Georgetown had won the Big East four times by beating Syracuse in the tournament final. Georgetown's Alonzo Mourning, named the tournament's Most Valuable Player, scored a game-high twenty-three points. But his individual effort couldn't overcome Syracuse, which pulled out the win, 56–54.

Pittsburgh and Connecticut battled throughout the 2002 Big East championship game, going into double overtime. Pitt tied the game with a layup at the end of regulation and knotted the score again at the end of the first overtime. In the second overtime, Connecticut finally pulled ahead and held on to win the game, 74–65.

The NCAA Tournament

Twenty-eight NCAA championship games have been played since the Big East was founded in 1979. Five of those games were won by teams that came from the Big East Conference. Louisville, currently a Big East team, won in 1980 and again in 1986, when the Cardinals were part of the Metro Conference.

All together, the sixteen teams currently in the Big East have won a total of ten NCAA championships. Connecticut, Cincinnati, and Louisville each have won two titles, while Georgetown, Syracuse, Villanova, and Marquette have won one apiece. Marquette won it all in 1977, as an independent team; Cincinnati won its championships in 1961 and 1962, playing in the Missouri Valley Conference.

Georgetown vs. North Carolina—1982

The 1982 NCAA tournament final between Georgetown and the North Carolina Tar Heels marked the first time since the conference's

Georgetown's Patrick Ewing shoots as Houston's Hakeem Olajuwon blocks in 1985.

founding that a team from the Big East made it into the championship game. Though John Thompson Jr.'s Hoyas lost in the final seconds, Georgetown wouldn't have to wait long before winning the Big East's first NCAA championship.

Georgetown vs. Houston—1984

The 1984 championship game between Georgetown and the University of Houston featured a matchup between Georgetown's Patrick Ewing and Houston's Hakeem Olajuwon, two of college basketball's most dominant centers. Houston had lost in the finals to NC State the year before, while Georgetown wanted a second chance after the loss in 1982. Led by Ewing, Georgetown won 84–75. Years later, Ewing and Olajuwon would meet again in the 1994 NBA Finals, with Olajuwon's Houston Rockets beating Ewing's New York Knicks.

Villanova vs. Georgetown—1985

The 1985 NCAA tournament defined the Big East as a dominant basketball conference. Three Big East teams—Villanova, Georgetown, and St. John's—made it to the Final Four. Georgetown, the clear tournament favorite, beat St. John's 77–59 to make it to the championship game against underdog Villanova. Villanova fell behind early but fought back to take a one-point lead into halftime. Wildcats star Ed Pinckney outscored Patrick Ewing, and Villanova made nine out of ten free-throw attempts in the second half. In the end, the plucky Villanova team hung on to win its first NCAA championship, 66–64.

Connecticut vs. Duke—1999

Despite multiple NCAA tournament trips, 1999 was the first year that Connecticut made it

Connecticut's Richard Hamilton looks for a shot against Duke's Shane Battier during the second half of the 2004 NCAA championship game.

into the championship game. The Huskies went 34–2 during the regular season and easily beat Ohio State in the Final Four to advance to the championship game. Duke, their finals opponent, was the top-ranked team in the nation. Connecticut's defense held Duke star Elton Brand to fifteen points, while timely shots by Richard "Rip" Hamilton and Khalid El-Amin kept the score close for the Huskies. El-Amin sealed Connecticut's first NCAA championship with a pair of free throws, making the final score 77–74.

CHAPTER 4
Shooting Stars: Players of the Big East

Big East coaches have given out the Big East Men's Basketball Player of the Year Award every year since 1980. It recognizes the player who shows excellence on the court throughout the entire season. The winner is chosen by a vote, and players have tied and shared the honor five times. Many notable players have won the award, from Georgetown legend Patrick Ewing to current NBA stars Richard Hamilton and Emeka Okafor. Apart from the award winners, many excellent Big East players have stood out, going on to careers in the NBA.

The Big East tournament often plays a factor in who wins the award. Georgetown's John Duren was named the first winner in 1980, following Georgetown's victory over Syracuse in the first Big East tournament. In 2002, Connecticut's Caron Butler and Pittsburgh's Brendin Knight tied for the award after battling each other in one of the greatest tournament final games in conference history.

Patrick Ewing— Georgetown

Patrick Ewing was the centerpiece of a Georgetown team that went to the NCAA championship game in 1982, 1984, and 1985. Ewing was named Big East Player of the Year in 1984 and 1985, tying both times with St. John's star Chris Mullin. In 1985, Ewing also was presented with the national Naismith College Player of the Year Award. He left Georgetown as the Hoyas' career leader in rebounds and blocked shots and ranking second in scoring. Ewing was the first pick in the 1985 NBA draft and won the league's Rookie of the Year Award in 1986. He played in the NBA from 1985 to 2002, going to the finals with the New York Knicks in 1994. Ewing played on eleven All-Star teams and was a member of the 1992 "Dream Team" that won a gold medal at the 1992 Olympics.

Patrick Ewing's great athleticism made him one of college basketball's best shot blockers ever.

Chris Mullin—St. John's

Chris Mullin is the only player in Big East history to win the Player of the Year Award three times, winning it outright in 1983 and

Syracuse star Derrick Coleman grabs yet another board in a 1989 Big East tournament game against Providence.

sharing the award with Georgetown's Patrick Ewing in 1984 and 1985. Mullin led St. John's to the 1985 Final Four, losing to Ewing's Georgetown Hoyas. That year, he won the John R. Wooden Award, given by the Los Angeles Athletic Club to the country's most outstanding college basketball player. Along with sharing two Player of the Year awards with Patrick Ewing, Mullin played with Ewing on the 1984 and 1992 Olympic basketball teams. Mullin was selected in the first round of the 1985 NBA draft and played in the NBA until 2000. As of 2007, he still held St. John's career scoring record.

Derrick Coleman— Syracuse

Derrick Coleman played for Syracuse from 1986 to 1990, taking the Orangemen to the NCAA finals in 1987. Coleman was named Big East Rookie of the Year that season and Big East Player of the Year in 1990. By the time he left Syracuse, he was the school's all-time leading rebounder and scorer. Coleman was the number-one pick in the 1990 NBA draft and played in the NBA until 2005. He was named to the Syracuse All-Century team in 2000, and the school retired his uniform number, 44, in 2006.

Ray Allen—Connecticut

One of the purest shooters the Big East has ever seen, Ray Allen earned first-team All-America status and was named the Big East Player of the Year after the 1995–1996 season. Allen went on to a stellar NBA career, shooting his way onto seven All-Star teams between 2000 and 2007. In 2007, the University of Connecticut retired Allen's jersey number, 34.

Alonzo Mourning— Georgetown

When Alonzo Mourning arrived at Georgetown University in 1988, many expected him to be the next Patrick Ewing. He didn't disappoint, leading the Hoyas to a 29–5 record in his first season and winning the Big East's Rookie of the Year Award. A complete player, Mourning dominated opponents both offensively and defensively. In 1992, he became the first Big East player to ever win the conference's Player of the Year, Defensive Player of the Year, and Tournament Player of the Year awards. Mourning went on to a highly successful NBA career, playing in seven All-Star games and helping the Miami Heat win an NBA championship in 2006.

As of 2007, Ray Allen held Connecticut's record for career three-point field goal shooting percentage.

Big East Award Winners, Through the 2006–2007 Season

John R. Wooden Player of the Year (awarded since 1976)
Chris Mullin, St. John's—1985
Walter Berry, St. John's—1986

Naismith Men's College Player of the Year Award (awarded since 1969)
Patrick Ewing, Georgetown—1985

NCAA Basketball Tournament Most Outstanding Player Award (awarded since 1939)
Patrick Ewing, Georgetown—1984
Ed Pinckney, Villanova—1985
Richard Hamilton, Connecticut—1999
Carmelo Anthony, Syracuse—2003
Emeka Okafor, Connecticut—2004

Big East Player of the Year
John Duren, Georgetown—1980
John Bagley, Boston College—1981
Dan Callandrillo, Seton Hall—1982
Chris Mullin, St. John's—1983
Chris Mullin, St. John's, and Patrick Ewing, Georgetown—1984 (tie)
Chris Mullin, St. John's, and Patrick Ewing, Georgetown—1985 (tie)
Walter Berry, St. John's—1986
Reggie Williams, Georgetown—1987
Charles D. Smith, Pittsburgh—1988
Charles E. Smith, Georgetown—1989
Derrick Coleman, Syracuse—1990
Billy Owens, Syracuse—1991
Alonzo Mourning, Georgetown—1992
Terry Dehere, Seton Hall—1993

Donyell Marshall, Connecticut—1994
Kerry Kittles, Villanova—1995
Ray Allen, Connecticut—1996
Pat Garrity, Notre Dame—1997
Richard Hamilton, Connecticut—1998
Richard Hamilton, Connecticut, and Tim James, Miami—1999 (tie)
Troy Murphy, Notre Dame—2000
Troy Murphy, Notre Dame, and Troy Bell, Boston College—2001 (tie)
Caron Butler, Connecticut, and Brandin Knight, Pittsburgh—2002 (tie)
Troy Bell, Boston College—2003
Emeka Okafor, Connecticut—2004
Hakim Warrick, Syracuse—2005
Randy Foye, Villanova—2006
Jeff Green, Georgetown—2007

John R. Wooden Legends of Coaching Award
Jim Calhoun, Connecticut (2005)
Jim Boeheim, Syracuse (2006)

Naismith Men's College Coach of the Year (awarded since 1987)
Ben Howland, Pittsburgh (2002)
Jay Wright, Villanova (2006)

Richard Hamilton—Connecticut

Richard "Rip" Hamilton played for Connecticut from 1996 to 1999. During those three seasons, he helped the Huskies win the Big East tournament in 1998 and 1999. He scored twenty-seven points against Duke to help Connecticut win the 1999 NCAA championship. Hamilton was the Big East's Player of the Year in both 1998 and 1999, sharing the 1999 honor with Miami's Tim James. Hamilton is second on Connecticut's career scoring list, with 2,039. He was chosen in the first round of the 1999 NBA draft and was a key member of the Detroit Pistons team that won the NBA championship in 2004.

Emeka Okafor—Connecticut

Emeka Okafor played a crucial part in Connecticut's push to the 2004 NCAA championship title. Okafor, who played at Connecticut from 2001 to 2004, averaged nineteen points per game for the Huskies in 2004 and led the entire nation in blocks. He helped Connecticut win two Big East tournament final games over Pittsburgh, in 2002 and 2004. In 2004, Okafor was named the tournament's Most Outstanding Player and was also named Big East Player of the Year. In the 2004 NCAA championship game, Okafor scored twenty-four points and grabbed fifteen rebounds as Connecticut beat Georgia Tech for its second championship in school history. Drafted by the Charlotte Bobcats, he was named NBA Rookie of the Year in 2005.

Other Star Players

Many other players have had great college careers, and several have gone on to have outstanding careers in pro basketball.

Mark Jackson played for St. John's from 1983 to 1987. In 1987, he set a school record for most assists in a career, with 326. Jackson was the 1987 NBA Rookie of the Year and played in the NBA until 2004. His 10,323 career assists rank him second all-time, behind John Stockton. After retiring from the NBA, Jackson went to work as a basketball analyst on television.

Sherman Douglas played point guard for the Syracuse Orangemen in the late 1980s, the most successful period in the school's history. In a 1989 game against Providence, Douglas dished out twenty-two assists, a Syracuse record. He finished with 960 career assists, an NCAA record at the time.

Dikembe Mutombo played at Georgetown from 1987 to 1991. A great shot blocker, he once set a Hoyas record by rejecting twelve shots in a single game. In the NBA, Mutombo was named NBA Defensive Player of the Year four times and has been an all-star eight times.

Allen Iverson spent only two years at Georgetown (1994–1996), but he was one of the Big East's greatest scorers. He scored 926 points in 1996, the most ever by a Georgetown player in a

Billy Donovan

Billy "The Kid" Donovan played for the Providence Friars from 1983 to 1987. In 1987, he averaged 20.6 points per game and led Providence to victory in the Southeast Regional of the NCAA tournament, winning the Most Valuable Player Award in the process. In the Final Four, Donovan's Friars lost to Big East rival Syracuse, but the scrappy guard made it clear that he was a winner. Donovan played briefly in the NBA before going on to become a highly successful college basketball coach. He led the University of Florida Gators of the Southeastern Conference to three NCAA championship games, winning consecutive national titles in 2006 and 2007.

single season. Iverson was named Big East Defensive Player of the Year for both of his seasons. He left Georgetown in 1996 for the NBA, going on to become one of professional basketball's most prominent stars.

Carmelo Anthony played just one season at Syracuse, leading the Orangemen to their first ever NCAA tournament championship in 2003. Anthony was a first-round pick by the Denver Nuggets in the 2003 NBA draft. In 2006, he became the second-youngest player to score 5,000 points, behind LeBron James.

Georgetown's Allen Iverson drives past Texas Tech's Jason Martin during the 1996 NCAA tournament.

School Spirit in the Big East

From Washington, D.C., to Wisconsin, team spirit is a huge part of what makes the Big East so special. Fans fill arenas wearing school colors and cheering on their teams' starting five. Many of the programs have mascots and courtside traditions that go back for decades; others are relatively new. With the recent conference expansion, some schools still are getting used to playing each other.

Georgetown Hoyas—Jack the Bulldog

Georgetown athletic teams were once called the Stonewalls. Stonewalls fans would shout the Latin phrase "Hoya Saxa!" which means, "What rocks!" The Hoyas nickname eventually grew out of the cheer. The team is represented by a bulldog mascot named Jack. The school used real bulldogs until the 1970s, when students started dressing up in blue and gray bulldog costumes. The Hoyas play at the Verizon Center, which seats more than 20,000 fans.

Syracuse Orange—Otto the Orange

Syracuse's first mascot was an invented Native American figure called the Saltine Warrior. He made his debut in 1931. After several protests by Native American groups, the Saltine Warrior was dropped in the 1970s. Today, Syracuse's mascot is an orange named Otto the Orange. At basketball games, Otto performs inside Syracuse's massive Carrier Dome. With a crowd capacity of 33,000, the Carrier Dome is the largest on-campus basketball arena in NCAA basketball.

Otto the Orange performs for fans during a 2004 game against Pittsburgh at Syracuse's Carrier Dome.

St. John's Red Storm— Thunder the Stallion

Sports teams at St. John's College were once called the Redmen because the school's athletic teams wore red. The nickname evolved to reflect Native American culture, including a mascot dressed as a warrior. The nickname was changed in 1994 to the Red Storm because the Redmen name and mascot came to be seen as negative stereotypes of Native Americans. St. John's kept red as its primary school color, however. St. John's teams are represented by a stallion mascot named Thunder. The men's basketball team plays home games at Madison Square Garden, home of the Big East tournament.

Connecticut Huskies— Jonathan the Husky

The University of Connecticut uses the husky—a type of sled dog—as its mascot. The choice seems natural, as the term "UConn" sounds just like Alaska's Yukon region, where sled dogs are common. UConn's sports teams have used real dogs as mascots since 1934, when the school's students chose the Husky mascot by a vote. All of the Huskies mascots are named Jonathan, after Jonathan Trumbull, Connecticut's first governor. All but the first husky have been white, with one blue eye and one brown eye. Their white coats and blue eyes match the school colors.

UConn's official mascot is a Siberian husky named Jonathan. A costumed mascot also makes appearances at games.

Seton Hall Pirates—Pirate

In 1931, Seton Hall University's baseball team defeated Holy Cross, inspiring a Massachusetts sportswriter to call them "a gang of pirates." The nickname caught on and has been in use ever since. Seton Hall plays home games at the Prudential Center in Newark, New Jersey, where a mascot in a pirate costume inspires the crowd. Seton Hall's colors are blue and white.

Villanova Wildcats— Wildcat

Villanova's Wildcat nickname dates back to 1926, when the school held a contest to pick a mascot for its athletic teams. The wildcat represents the players' fierceness, agility, and alertness. Villanova's wildcat mascot most closely resembles a bobcat. The school used caged, live bobcats for a while, but it switched to a person in a wildcat costume in 1950. Called Will D. Cat, the mascot wears a Villanova jersey of blue and white, the school's colors.

Providence Friars—Friar and Dalmatian

Villanova mascot Will D. Cat encourages the home crowd at Philadelphia's 21,000-seat Wachovia Center.

Similar to some other schools in the Big East, Providence College has ties to the Catholic Church. Its nickname reflects the fact that the school is run by Dominican priests, who are also known as friars. Providence College's logo shows a friar wearing the Dominicans' traditional black cowl, which is a hooded, robe-like garment. In 1993, Providence revived the practice of using a Dalmatian as a mascot. Like the canine, Providence's school colors are black and white. The Friars play their home games off campus at the Dunkin' Donuts Center, known locally as "the Dunk."

Pittsburgh Panthers—Roc the Panther

Pittsburgh's panther mascot takes the name "Roc" from the famous Pittsburgh football player and coach Steve Petro. His fifty-year involvement with Pittsburgh sports led some to call him "the rock" upon which the Pitt football program was built. The school named its panther mascot Roc in Petro's honor. Roc wears a Vegas gold and navy jersey to represent the school, and the mascot sings, dances, and inspires fans at the Peterson Events Center, which is popularly called "the Pete."

Notre Dame Fighting Irish—Leprechaun

No one knows for certain how Notre Dame's teams got the Fighting Irish nickname. One theory is that it came from Irish immigrants who fought in the American Civil War. Among them was Notre Dame's third president, Father William Corby. Sportswriters first popularized the nickname in the 1920s, in newspaper columns about the school's famed football team. Early on, Notre Dame's teams used Irish terrier dogs with various names as their mascots. In 1965, they officially adopted the Leprechaun. The enthusiastic student who earns the right to be the Leprechaun wears a green suit with a gold vest and a green hat to represent the school colors. The Fighting Irish play at the Edmund P. Joyce Center, in South Bend, Indiana.

West Virginia Mountaineers—The Mountaineer

West Virginia University started using the mountaineer as a mascot in 1936. The mountaineer represents the tough frontier settlers who lived in the state's mountains. The mascot wears a fringed brown leather jacket and coonskin cap and carries a mock rifle. Male mascots traditionally grow beards to go along with the rugged-looking costume. Unlike many college mascots, the mountaineer does not use the school's colors, which are blue and gold.

Rutgers Scarlet Knights —Scarlet Knight

Rutgers University was one of the first schools to compete in inter-collegiate sports, dating to an 1866 baseball game. Scarlet was adopted officially as a school color in 1900. Rutgers took "Scarlet Knights" as its nickname in 1955. The first Scarlet Knight mascot appeared that same year. Rutgers plays at the Louis Brown Athletic Center, which is also known as "the RAC" (Rutgers Athletic Center).

The West Virginia Mountaineer dances for fans during a 2007 Big East tournament game against Providence.

Cincinnati Bearcats—Bearcat

The Bearcats' nickname dates to a 1914 football game. Cincinnati's star player was named Leonard K. "Teddy" Baehr. During the game, a cheerleader inspired the crowd to chant "Come on, Baehr-cat!" The next day, a cartoonist for the student newspaper drew a picture of a large cat with a bear's head to represent the team. By the 1920s, the nickname had caught on. The Cincinnati Bearcats play their home games on campus at the Fifth Third Arena. The school's colors are red and black.

DePaul Blue Demons

The DePaul Blue Demon nickname came about in 1922. At the time, the school's teams actually didn't have a name, just a blue "D" used on the front of players' jerseys. A local newspaper writer called them the D-men, which quickly caught on with fans. DePaul football coach Frank Haggarty changed it slightly to Blue Demons and officially adopted it that year. Named Dibs the Blue Demon, the horned, devilish mascot dresses in DePaul's royal blue and scarlet colors and represents the fun and spirit of the school's sports teams. The Blue Demons play at the Allstate Arena in Chicago.

Marquette Golden Eagles—Golden Eagle

Marquette University's sports teams played as the Golden Warriors from 1954 to 1994, when the nickname was changed to the Golden Eagles. The nickname was changed briefly to Gold, but it was changed back to Golden Eagles in 2005 after protests by students and fans. Today, the teams are represented by a mascot in an eagle costume. Marquette's colors are blue and gold.

Louisville Cardinals— Cardinal Bird

The University of Louisville wanted a nickname that would identify it with Kentucky. Administrators felt that the best representative would be the cardinal, Kentucky's state bird. The nickname was adopted around 1913, as were the school colors—red, black, and white. The Cardinal costume and logo depict a snarling, fierce-looking bird. The Cardinals play home games off campus at Freedom Hall, which has a 19,000-seat capacity.

The Cardinal's mascot whips up the Louisville faithful during the first round of the 2004 NCAA tournament.

South Florida Bulls— Rocky the Bull

Shortly after the University of South Florida was founded in 1956, the school had a contest to choose a mascot. The Golden Brahmins—referring to a breed of cattle—was the winning selection. The mascot was unveiled officially in 1962. In the 1980s, the school decided to simplify the nickname to the Bulls. Rocky the Bull dates to the 1982 name change.

GLOSSARY

alignment Grouping or positioning of teams, as in a conference or league.

athletic conference Association of sports teams that play against each other competitively.

boon Benefit or blessing.

collegiate Pertaining to or connected with a college or colleges.

commissioner Administrative head of a sports league.

consecutive Occurring one after the other.

consolation game In a tournament, a game held between the two losing semifinalists to determine third and fourth place.

elite The best of a class.

enthusiastic Energetic and excited.

expansion An increase in size or number; enlargement.

playoffs Games played in order to determine a championship.

plucky Spirited, brave.

prestigious Highly respected.

rebounding In basketball, grabbing or taking possession of a missed shot.

semifinal One of the two games in the second-to-last round of a tournament.

stereotype Figure or concept that represents an oversimplified opinion.

stint Period of time spent at a particular activity.

FOR MORE INFORMATION

Big East Conference
222 Richmond Street, Suite 110
Providence, RI 02903
(401) 272-9108
Web site: http://www.bigeast.org

Los Angeles Athletic Club
431 West 7th Street
Los Angeles, CA 90014
(213) 625-2211
E-mail: laac@laac.net
Web site: http://www.laac.com

Naismith Basketball Hall of Fame
1000 West Columbus Avenue
Springfield, MA 01105
(413) 781-6500
E-mail: mburns@hoophall.com
Web site: http://www.hoophall.com

National Association of Basketball Coaches
1111 Main Street, Suite 1000
Kansas City, MO 64105-2136
(816) 878-6222
Web site: http://nabc.cstv.com

National Collegiate Athletic Association
700 W. Washington Street

P.O. Box 6222
Indianapolis, IN 46206-6222
(317) 917-6222
Web site: http://www.ncaa.org

National Invitation Tournament
60 East 42nd Street, Suite 660
New York, NY 10165-0015
(212) 425-6510
Web site: http://www.nit.org

Web Sites

Due to the changing nature of Internet links, the Rosen Publishing Group, Inc., has developed an online list of Web sites related to the subject of this book. This site is updated regularly. Please use this link to access the list:

http://www.rosenlinks.com/imcb/bbec

Einhorn, Eddie, and Ron Rappaport. *How March Became Madness*. Chicago, IL: Triumph Books, 2006.

Fulks, Matt, ed. *CBS Sports Presents: Stories from the Final Four*. Lenexa, KS: Addax Publishing Group, 2002.

Johnson, Gary K., ed. *Official 2007 NCAA Men's Final Four Records Book*. Chicago, IL: Triumph Books, 2006.

Johnson, Gary K., et al., eds. *NCAA Men's Basketball Records Book*. Chicago, IL: Triumph Books, 2006.

Kerkhoff, Blair. *Greatest Book of College Basketball*. Lenexa, KS: Addax, 2002.

Pinckney, Ed, and Mike Gordon. *Ed Pinckney's Tales from the Villanova Hardwood*. New York, NY: Sports Publishing, 2004.

Stewart, Mark. *Final Four*. New York, NY: Franklin Watts, 2002.

Waters, Mike. *Legends of Syracuse Basketball*. New York, NY: Sports Publishing, 2004.

Wyszkowski, Rob, ed. *NCAA March Madness*. Chicago, IL: Triumph Books, 2004.

BIBLIOGRAPHY

Big East Conference. "2006–07 Men's Basketball Media Guide." 2006. Retrieved June 15, 2007 (http://www.bigeast.org/sports/m-baskbl/spec-rel/06-07-bige-mbb-guide.html).

Calhoun, Jim, and Leigh Montville. *Dare to Dream: Connecticut Basketball's Remarkable March to the National Championship.* New York, NY: Broadway Books, 1999.

Davis, Barker. "Pitino Returns to His Roots; Louisville Coach Is Back in Big East." *Washington Times.* November 18, 2005. Retrieved June 15, 2007 (http://www.washingtontimes.com/sports/20051118-122026-8557r.htm).

Feinstein, John. *A Season on the Brink.* New York, NY: Simon & Schuster, 1989.

Feinstein, John. *Last Dance: Behind the Scenes at the Final Four.* New York, NY: Little, Brown and Company, 2006.

McNamara, Kevin. "Big East Influx in Hoop Hall of Fame." *Providence Journal.* September 10, 2005. Retrieved June 15, 2007 (http://www.projo.com/college/content/projo_20050910_10hall.d0c7717.html).

Pells, Eddie. "Big East Sues in Attempt to Stop ACC Expansion." Associated Press. June 6, 2003. Retrieved June 15, 2007 (http://www.centralohio.com/ohiostate/stories/20030606/football/433381.html).

Savage, Jim. *The Encyclopedia of the NCAA Basketball Tournament.* New York, NY: Dell Publishing, 1990.

Wilbon, Michael. "25 Years Ago: Jordan, Worthy, Ewing, Oh My!" *Washington Post.* March 25, 2007. Retrieved June 1, 2007 (http://www.washingtonpost.com/wp-dyn/content/article/2007/03/24/AR2007032401106.html).

INDEX

About the Author

Jason Porterfield has authored more than twenty books for Rosen Publishing on topics ranging from U.S. history to the environment. His books on sports subjects include *Kurt Busch: NASCAR Driver*; *Baseball: Rules, Tips, Strategy, and Safety*; and *Basketball in the ACC (Atlantic Coast Conference)*. Porterfield currently lives in Chicago.

Photo Credits

Cover top, pp. 4–5, 7, 15, 18, 33, 35, 37, 39, 41 © Getty Images; cover bottom, pp. 13, 24 © Georgetown University Sports Information; p. 3 (left) © www.istockphoto.com/Benjamin Goode; pp. 6, 10–11, 12, 19, 26, 34 © www.istockphoto.com; pp. 8, 14, 30, 32 © www.istockphoto.com/Bill Grove; pp. 9, 29, 36 © University of Connecticut; pp. 17, 20, 25, 28 © AP Photos; p. 22 © St. John's University; p. 27 © Focus on Sport/Getty Images.

Designer: Tom Forget; **Editor:** Christopher Roberts
Photo Researcher: Marty Levick